SUMMARY

OF

THE FOUR AGREEMENTS

A PRACTICAL GUIDE TO PERSONAL FREEDOM

(A Toltec Wisdom Book)

By

DON MIGUEL RUIZ

Quick Reads

NOTE

This book is a summary and analysis and is meant as a companion to, not a replacement for the original book. Quick Reads is wholly responsible for this content and not associated with the original author in any way.

Legal Note

This book or its parts thereof may not be reproduced in any form, stored in any retrieval system, or distributed in any format by any means be it electronic, mechanical, photocopy, recording, or otherwise without any written permission of the publisher, except as provided by United States of America copyright law.

Disclaimer

All materials in this book are for educational and informational purposes only. We accept no responsibility for any effects or results obtained from the use of this material.

Although every effort has been made to provide correct and adequate information, the author assumes no responsibility for the accuracy, use, or misuse of such information.

Copyright © 2021 by Quick Reads.
All Rights Reserved.

Table of Contents

BRIEF CONTENT

DON MIGUEL RUIZ'S PERSPECTIVE

WHAT'S IN IT FOR ME & WHY IS IT IMPORTANT?

INTRODUCTION

THE OUTSIDE WORLD NEGATIVELY DOMESTICATES YOU.

YOU LIVE IN A DREAM

BUT IT'S A DREAM YOU CAN WAKE UP FROM

ACCEPTING DEATH IS AS IMPORTANT AS ACCEPTING LIFE.

AWARENESS IS THE STARTING POINT OF YOUR JOURNEY.

WHEN YOU DEVELOP AWARENESS, YOU'LL DEVELOP FORGIVENESS.

IF YOU CAN FORGIVE, YOU CAN ACT.

WE ALL LIVE IN OUR OWN DREAM.

BE IMPECCABLE WITH YOUR WORD

DON'T TAKE ANYTHING PERSONALLY.

DON'T MAKE ASSUMPTIONS

ALWAYS DO YOUR BEST

3 MOST FASCINATING LESSONS YOU NEED TO KNOW

Lesson One
Lesson Two
Lesson Three
Awareness
Discipline
Dead

CONCLUSION

WHO SHOULD READ THIS BOOK?

Brief Content

The Four Agreements is a book by Don Miguel Ruiz, subtitled as: a practical guide to personal freedom. Don Miguel was apprenticed to a shaman and has extensive knowledge of the ancient Toltecs. The Toltecs were natives of the Mexican culture of great warriors and artists who lived around 1000 years ago. This revolutionary book is based on the Toltec belief of freedom from self-limiting beliefs that can cause suffering in a person's life.

The Four Agreements is a very influential book. It was first published in 1997 and has become a popular book again since the approval of the book by Oprah Winfrey in 2001 and 2013. Ever since then, it has been translated into 46 languages, over 8.2 million copies sold in the United States alone, and has been on the New York Times bestseller list for over a decade.

Don Miguel Ruiz's Perspective

Don Miguel Ruiz is a popular Mexican writer whose work is built around the Toltec spiritualist and neo-shamanic texts of the Toltecs. He uses ancient teachings to seek spiritual enlightenment. In 2018, he was listed among Warkin's 100 Most Spiritually Influential People.

What's In It For Me & Why Is It Important?

After reading this book, The Four Agreements, you'll discover that we have been tamed "domesticated" from childhood, how these internal rules harm you and what you can do to break and replace them to a new agreement with yourself.

You will also discover:

* *What the word impeccable truly means*

* *How a mother can ruin her daughter's life with one sentence*

* *The reason daydreaming is a bad idea*

* *What makes questions so important*

* *Why it means something different to do your best every day*

What people say and do to you is a reflection on them, not on you

Three ways to break your old agreements and live with the new ones chosen by you.

Introduction

I am fascinated by ancient cultures, especially those that were far ahead of their time, like the Spartans, Romans, and Egyptians. Unfortunately, we rarely consider South America in this regard, but it has been home to many of these ancient and advanced civilizations.

The Aztecs had a super-efficient farming system and built the foundation of Mexico City. The Mayans are known for their incredibly precise calendar and one of the New Seven Wonders of the World. One culture which is rarely mentioned but which contains a lot of wisdom is the Toltec. Mexican surgeon and author Don Miguel Ruiz, who went from science to spirituality after a near-fatal car crash, knows all about it.

Don Miguel Ruiz's 1997 book, The Four Agreements was comfortably on the New York Times bestseller list for eight years, sold about 8.200,000 copies, and publicizing these four guiding principles:

1. Be impeccable with your word.

2. Don't take anything personally.

3. Don't make assumptions.

4. Always do your best.

Today, through this summary, you'll know why we need them, which is most important and how you can work to make them a part of your life.

Let's dive in!

The Outside World Negatively Domesticates You.

"Our biggest fear is not dying, it's being ourselves."

~ Don Miguel Ruiz

In this actionable book, Don Miguel proves to us that the outside world has a vast influence on how we live our lives. Don Miguel calls this domestication. Domestication is generally not very positive. Instead, it forces us to be afraid and make judgments. We become obsessed with the rewards because we are punished for bad deeds and rewarded for obeying the world around us. This is not good for us because it teaches us how to take good steps to get rewards. We should pursue good deeds before the action itself. The punishment for not obeying makes us feel like we are not good enough. On this basis, Don Miguel believes that our greatest fear in life is not death. Instead, our greatest fear is being who we really are. So, to be truly happy, we have to break free from our bonds.

These bonds develop at a young age. We are born into societal norms that dictate the dreams we can have in life. The collective dream of the planet affects our individual dreams. Our parents, religions, schools, and politicians taught us this collective dream. Through this training, we learn to behave "correctly," what to believe, and the difference between right and wrong. Our acceptance of these societal agreements has to be called our domestication. We often get oppressed and punished in our childhood or adolescence by stronger parents and teachers if we tried to rebel. Just as animals, we have also been rewarded for obeying these more powerful individuals. Then we all gave up and decided to follow the collective dream instead of our individual dreams. Though as we get older, we don't need a stronger person to domesticate and control us. These ideas are designed to domesticate us. Don Miguel suggests that we can step out of this structure and make new agreements for ourselves. These are the four agreements.

You Live In A Dream

"Ninety-five percent of the beliefs we have stored in our minds are nothing but lies, and we suffer because we believe all the lies."

~ Don Miguel Ruiz

Don Miguel believes that domestication leads us all to live in a dream. We base our decisions on irrational and false assumptions about ourselves. We grow up blaming and judging ourselves and others. We also strive for rewards based on a system we didn't even choose.

But It's A Dream You Can Wake Up From

The most vital thing is that it is possible to wake up from this dream. It is possible to reshape your reality without the endless pursuit of improvement. A life without suffering is possible.

In other to do this, you are required to master these three skills:

1. **Awareness**: you must be aware that you're living in a dream-like state full of illusions; see these illusions for what they are.

2. **Forgiveness**: then you have to accept the consequences of these illusions; how illusions affect you and the people around you.

3. **Action:** You need to dissolve this dream now and turn it into something more realistic.

If you could master these three skills, you would have achieved enlightenment. It is a time without suffering and can also be called the second awakening.

Accepting Death Is As Important As Accepting Life.

We have to accept death, and the concept of death will teach us how to live our life. When we honestly think about death, we can accept that life does not last forever. When we accept this, we care less about what other people think and live our life the way we want to. By listening to the angels of death, we can live in the present as much as possible. We can enjoy life without being tied to the concept of life.

Awareness Is The Starting Point Of Your Journey.

Don Miguel says we should be aware that our life is like a dream. He also wants us to accept that death is essential to our lives. However, we need to be aware to realize that our life is like a dream and that one day we will die. However, your awareness may fade over the course of your life. For a moment, you are no longer in a dream state. So, you don't know how you live anymore. Therefore, in addition to developing awareness, we must also learn to maintain awareness. Train your awareness like a muscle. This is the sole way to achieve true and consistent enlightenment.

Two great ways to raise and uphold your awareness are meditation and fasting. Buddha opened a clear path for meditation, fasting, and mindfulness. Don Miguel urges us to follow in his footsteps. Don Miguel also points out that an herbal tradition is extremely important. Plants have changed everyone's experience. Native American shamanic practices lead to this suggestion.

When You Develop Awareness, You'll Develop Forgiveness.

The forgiveness that Don Miguel associates with awareness is forgiving our past and our continued failures against the agreements we still have. There is also forgiveness for ourselves and the environment that suffer because of our accepted delusions. Also, forgiveness for the suffering that others cause because of their dreams.

Don Miguel believes that universal love is based on the acceptance of all. When you are ready to accept the world and the people around you, you will feel a huge increase in weight off your shoulders.

This increased acceptance does not mean that you will always meet your expectations. Instead, you will fail, and so will the others. But accepting these mistakes and accepting that we are only humans will help you stay aware.

If You Can Forgive, You Can Act.

Don Miguel emphasizes that forgiveness frees up the space, energy, and strength necessary to change your reality in all four agreements. *Forgiveness encourages three actions:*

* *Prevent new unwanted agreements from taking root*

* *Eliminate harmful old agreements that already exist*

* *Program new agreements that will gradually eliminate suffering*

We All Live In Our Own Dream.

We must accept not only our dream-like life but also understand others. Don Miguel Ruiz points out that we are not responsible for others; we are only accountable for ourselves. When we accept that we are no longer accountable for others, we will no longer be hurt by the actions of others. We act less personally against ourselves when we know that others are only acting based on their own dream-like lives. Don Miguel describes it as immune to the emotional poison of others. If you avoid this emotional poison, you can easily move around the world.

By not taking things personally, we also gain the ability to trust our hearts more to control our lives. They are less controlled by the opinions and actions of others. Your objective reality will guide you.

Based on all these ideas, Don Miguel presented four clear ideas that should be implemented.

Be Impeccable With Your Word

"The big difference between a warrior and a victim is that the victim represses and the warrior refrains."

~ Don Miguel Ruiz

Don Miguel says that this first agreement is the most vital but often also the most difficult to keep. He points out that the word impeccable "faultless" has its origin from the Latin word for sin and a Latin prefix for "without". Don Miguel explains that sin is all that contradicts you. Therefore, being blameless "impeccable" with your word means taking responsibility for your actions and not being judgmental. Non-judgmental towards others and yourself. Don Miguel illustrates words as more powerful than we think. These are the building blocks of labels, concepts, and beliefs. Therefore, we have to be careful before using words because we can create new harmful illusions. The most easiest way to do this is to get into the habit of just saying what you mean and only meaning what you say. Don't say anything if you're not sure.

Don't Take Anything Personally.

"Comments are a reflection of the commentator's reality, not yours."

~ Don Miguel Ruiz

As mentioned earlier, by not taking things personally, you can avoid being hurt by harmful treatment. It keeps you from absorbing the words of others. Having a solid sense of self-worth means that you don't have to trust the opinions of others to feel content or satisfied. We need to become less responsive and move away from the actions of others. We have to realize that if we were in that person's reality, so would we. Don Miguel believes that anger, jealousy, envy, and sadness can go away if we stop taking things personally.

Don Miguel also clarifies that taking things personally can lead to Personal importance. Personal importance is a state in which we believe everything revolves around us, which makes us take things more personally. Ultimately, you end up in a cycle of worrying about what other people think.

Don Miguel reminds readers that absolutely nothing that people say or do to you concerns you. Instead, all of their actions are absolutely about them. Insults are often associated with personal issues or with a person's beliefs. Therefore, Don Miguel suggests not to solicit information from others, as their views are never relevant. Instead, focus on yourself and getting better.

Don't Make Assumptions

"Find the courage to ask questions and to express what you really want. Communicate with others as clearly as you can to avoid misunderstandings, sadness, and drama."

~ Don Miguel Ruiz

In Don Miguel's eyes, assumptions lead to suffering. Assumptions often have little basis in reality and are only real in our imagination. Thinking about the thoughts of others can cause stress or conflict. Oftentimes, people will see their assumption as the truth, which is why assumptions usually lead to negative consequences. To overcome this expectation, Don Miguel suggests asking questions and maintaining clear communication with others. This transparent communication prevents assumptions from sticking. Don Miguel says that following this agreement will help you avoid misunderstanding, heartache, and drama. The easiest way to build this agreement into your life is to keep the following in mind: If someone or something surprises you, failure isn't theirs; it's yours.

Uncontrolled assumptions can often hurt our relationships. For instance, people often assume that their partners know what they are thinking. Then people believe their partners are going to do whatever they want. When they don't, they are often disappointed or angry with their partner. So again, Don Miguel suggests that we ask more questions to be successful.

Always Do Your Best

"Enjoy the path and the destination will take care of itself."

~ Don Miguel Ruiz

Doing your best doesn't necessarily mean doing the best that is physically possible. It means doing the best you can manage individually, which can vary depending on the situation and your current situation. One way to do your best is to incorporate the previous three agreements into your daily life. This way, you can avoid feeling regret and accept that people are doing their best all the time. You will start enjoying the action itself instead of just enjoying the rewards of the action. Likewise, Don Miguel suggests that we should work hard because it makes us happier than external motivation. Don Miguel gives an example of salaries. If the primary motivation for our work is money, we will never do our best. We will also find ourselves stuck in high-paying jobs that lack satisfaction and happiness. Due to the lack of job satisfaction, these people tend to spend their weekends partying, drinking, and doing other things that might take a toll on their lives.

If you do your best to work hard because you enjoy the task, your job will seem easy. That way, the final agreement - to always do your best - will increase the strength of all other agreements and help you break free.

3 Most Fascinating Lessons You Need To Know

Lesson one

Our environment domesticates us right from infancy which leads us to an unwise life.

There are many areas of our life that we don't choose or control. Don Miguel Ruiz calls the sum of this "domestication". It is a process that begins on the day we are born. You don't choose your first language, you don't choose your first school, and you can't control the attitudes your parents teach you.

Parents, peers, teachers, religion, all of these influences teach us a set of rules. As children, we do not have power over them. We are rewarded when we do good and punished when we think outside the box. Combine that for almost two decades, and you will be someone who seeks benefits, is afraid of rejection, and doesn't question the rules of society.

The worst part about this collective dream, as Ruiz calls it, is that at some point, we will be so tamed that we will continue to do it ourselves. If you've ever broken a rule, such as: For example, if you missed a deadline and were mentally punished, judged, and blamed yourself, you've seen this problem in action.

How to break out of this circle? With new agreements!

Lesson Two

What people say or do to you is nothing personal, but you must know who you are to be okay with it.

One of the new internal rules that you must follow is to take nothing personally. It's the second of four agreements, and I think it's the strongest. I recently explained this to a friend over dinner.

Nothing, absolutely nothing that others and the world do or tell you is relevant to you. When a person calls you ugly, it says a lot more about them and their issues than it does about you. Whatever problems they have, they got them to express their frustration.

Whether it is true or not, taking it personally means acknowledging it, and it means - to some extent - believing it. You should, therefore, never take anything personally. But it's hard not to take hurtful comments and setbacks personally.

According to Ruiz, the unique way to really get into this habit is to become very self-aware. Once you know very deep who you are, what your truth is, and that you are good enough, you can stop looking for validation and acceptance.

Lesson Three

There are three ways you can use to break old agreements, break free, and make your own.

Can you see how great such a new agreement might be if you really cling to it? Of course, there are many waiting to be learned. But to make such a big difference, you must first break free from the shackles of your old domesticated system to these three fundamental paths to freedom: Awareness, Discipline and Dead

The Three Fundamental Paths To Freedom As Suggested By Don Miguel Ruiz:

Awareness
* Start noticing the fear-based beliefs that are making you miserable. We all have them. Our attention has been focused on them since childhood, and we could not have developed them. Now it's time to let beliefs go and move on.

Discipline
* Learn to let go and forgive those who have hurt you, especially yourself. The Toltecs christened this

the parasite in your mind. An argument, a missed bus, a spilled glass of milk, anything that triggers negative emotions, can trigger a downward spiral and ruin your day. If you don't forgive yourself and everyone involved. It's the only thing you can do now to be able to move on instantly.

Dead

* Remember that each day can be the last that remains in the present.

The initiation of the dead creates clarity. How do you want to live? Do you truly want to let the opinion of others control what you do now?

Conclusion

It all takes time, repeated practice, and finding a way to make them work for you, but these are the starting points for getting rid of the clutter in your mind and finally starting to live on your own terms.

Who Should Read This Book?

The 18-year-old dancer, who's struggling with her mom's negative comments, the 33-year-old actor/actress, who constantly has to deal with people's personal feedback, and anyone having a hard time saying sorry.

HOW DO WE BECOME WISER?

"Wisdom is a virtue that isn't innate, but can only be acquired through experience. Anyone who is interested in trying new things and reflecting on the process has the ability to gain wisdom. By learning as much as you can, analyzing your experiences and putting your knowledge to the test, you can become a wiser person".

~ mooshwalks

Did you like the wisdom you've learned here? Check out our related and other fascinating books by searching on Amazon:

(Summary by quick reads)

QUICK READS

We're just scratching the surface here. If you don't already have the original book, "**The Four Agreements:** *A Practical Guide to Personal Freedom (A Toltec Wisdom Book)* by **Don Miguel Ruiz**", order it here on Amazon to learn the juicy details.

Printed in Great Britain
by Amazon